My toys

Toys and numbers

1

1 Read. Then match.

 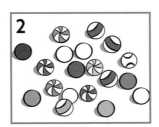  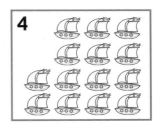

a fourteen boats   **b** eleven kites   **c** nineteen balls   **d** sixteen dolls

2 Read. Then match.

T0344355

1 twenty-three	**a**	14
2 eighteen	**b**	18
3 thirty-one	**c**	23
4 fourteen	**d**	31
5 forty-seven	**e**	47

3 Write. Then match.

1 How many trains are there?

There are ___twenty-two___ trains.

2 How many teddy bears are there?

_____

3 How many bikes are there?

_____

4 How many cars are there?

_____

a 15

b 40

c 22

d 12

4 Write questions and answers.

1

What's this?

It's a boat.

2

_____

_____

3

_____

_____

4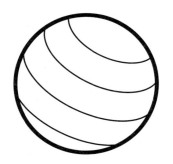

_____

_____

5 Read the answers. Then write the questions and draw.

1 <u>What are these?</u>   They're books.

  <u>How many books are there?</u>   There are three.

2 _____   It's a bus.

_____   There's one.

3 _____   They're lorries.

_____   There are two.

6 Look, read and write. Use words from the box.

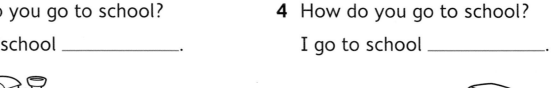

by train   ~~by bike~~   by bus   by car

1 How do you go to school?

  I go to school <u>by bike</u>.

2 How do you go to school?

  I go to school _____.

3 How do you go to school?

  I go to school _____.

4 How do you go to school?

  I go to school _____.

7 **Unscramble. Then write and answer.**

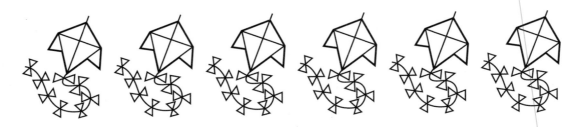

| kites | there | How | are | ? | many |

1 How many kites are there?
There are six.

| many | are | ? | How | dolls | there |

2 _____

_____

| there | teddy bears | many | ? | are | How |

3 _____

_____

8 Read. Then colour.

Dear Aunt Emma,

Thank you for my boat. I love boats! I've got two boats —
a blue boat from you and a red boat from my friend Tina!

I've got a green bike from Mum and Dad and six blue dolls
from Granny and Grandad. And I've got a teddy bear from
my sister Rachel.

Thank you!
Love from
Anne x

9 Read again. Then circle *Yes* or *No*.

1 There are two boats. (Yes) / No

2 Aunt Emma's boat is red. Yes / No

3 The bike is green. Yes / No

4 There are five dolls. Yes / No

5 Rachel is Anne's friend. Yes / No

Remember!

We start a letter with Dear. We use a capital letter for the letter D and for the name.

We end a letter with From or Love from.

10 Read. Then circle.

1 *dear* / (Dear) Granny

2 *love* / *Love* from Pete

3 Dear *sandra* / *Sandra*

4 Love from *ken* / *Ken*

11 Write a thank-you letter.

- Who is the letter to?
- What is the toy?

- What colour is it?
- Do you like it?

Dear _____ ,

Thank you for the _____ .

It's _____ .

I _____ .

Love from

_____

My family

Who are they?

1 Look and read. Then answer. Use words from the word box.

cousins   brother   sister   aunt   ~~uncle~~

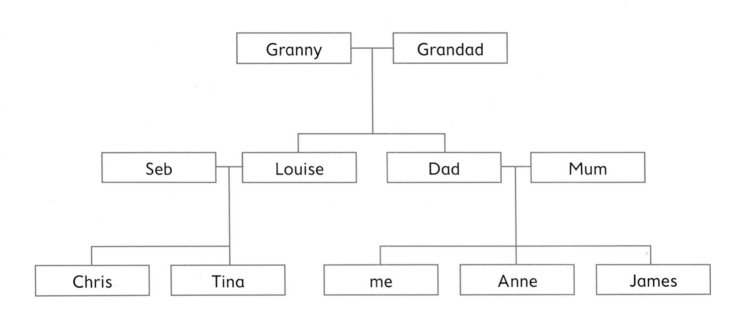

1 Who's Seb?   He's my uncle. _____

2 Who's James?   _____

3 Who's Louise?   _____

4 Who's Anne?   _____

5 Who are Tina and Chris?   _____

2 Look and match.

1	my uncle	**a**	living room
2	my brother	**b**	kitchen
3	my sister	**c**	bedroom
4	my granny	**d**	bathroom

3 Look and read. Then write.

1 Where's my uncle? _____

2 _____ She's in the bedroom.

3 Where's my granny? _____

4 _____ He's in the bathroom.

4 Where are they? Look and write.

1 Where are my parents?

They're in the attic.

_____

2 Where are my grandparents?

_____

_____

3 Where is the baby?

_____

_____

4 Where are the children?

_____

_____

5 **Look, read and write. Use words from the box.**

in ~~behind~~ next to on

1 My bed is ___behind___ the table.

2 My teddy bear is _____ the bathroom.

3 My lamp is _____ the table

4 The bathroom is _____ the bedroom.

6 **Read and draw on the picture in Activity 5.**

1 My kite is behind the bed.

2 My ball is under the bed.

3 My book is on my bed.

4 My boat is next to my teddy bear.

7 Look and read about Gill's family. Who is six years old?

My family

This is my mum. She's thirty-five. She's got straight hair.

This is my little sister, Jane. She's six years old.

This is my brother, Dan. He's on a chair.

This is Uncle Jon. He's in the kitchen

This is my aunt Maggie. She lives in Australia.

This is my cousin Bob. He's ten.

8 Read again. Then match.

1 Dan is Gill's   a aunt.

2 Maggie is Gill's   b uncle.

3 Bob is Gill's   c brother.

4 Jon is Gill's   d sister.

5 Jane is Gill's   e cousin.

2 Family

Remember!

cousin = boy or girl

9 **Write the names of four people in your family.**

1 _____ 2 _____

3 _____ 4 _____

10 **Draw pictures of the people in Activity 8. Then write.**

My family

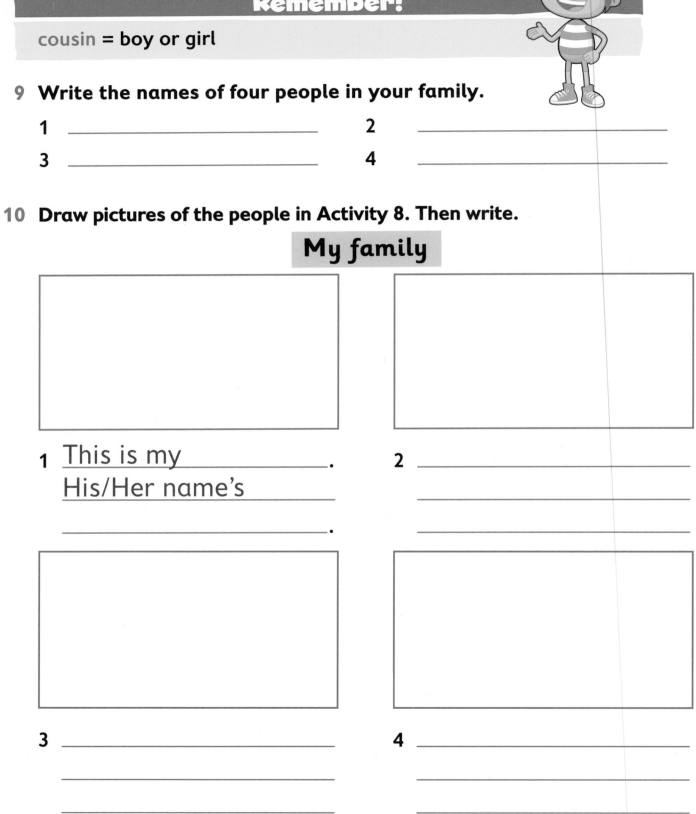

1 This is my _____.
His/Her name's _____
_____.

2 _____
_____
_____

3 _____
_____
_____

4 _____
_____
_____

1 Match the words.

| 1 point | 2 nod | 3 stamp | 4 clap | 5 touch |

| a your feet | b your head | c your hands | d your toes | e your fingers |

2 Look, read and circle.

1 **swing** / swim
2 do the splits / do cartwheels
3 stand on your head / catch a ball
4 throw a ball / climb

3 **Write *a*, *i* or *o*. Then match.**

1 st <u>a</u> nd ————
2 d _
3 cl _ p
4 st _ mp
5 thr _ w

a your hands
b on your head
c a ball
d your feet
e the splits

4 **What can they do? What can't they do? Look, then write.**

1 He <u>can</u> skip.

2 She _____ swim.

3 He _____ touch his toes.

4 She _____ dance.

5 Look. Then unscramble and write.

1 ball / I / a / kick / can

I can kick a ball.

2 can / I / the / splits / do

_____

3 can / head / stand / my / I / on

_____

4 fast / run / can / I

_____

5 high / can't / jump / I

_____

6 **Complete the questions. Then look and answer.**

	swim	climb	swing	do cartwheels	stand on your head
Mum	✔	✔	✘	✔	✔
Dad	✔	✔	✔	✘	✘
Granny	✔	✘	✔	✘	✘
Grandad	✔	✔	✘	✘	✘

1 ___Can___ Granny do cartwheels?

No, she can't. _____

2 _____ Grandad swing?

_____

3 _____ Mum climb?

_____

4 _____ Dad stand on his head?

_____

5 _____ Granny swim?

_____

7 **Write sentences with *can't*.**

1 Grandad can't stand on his head. _____

2 Granny _____.

3 Mum _____.

4 Dad _____.

5 I _____.

8 **What activities can you do at school?**
For example, can you swim? Can you climb?

_____

_____

9 **Read the index of this book about exercise. Then write.**

Index	
catch a ball .... page 11	pull .... page 1
do cartwheels .... page 14	push .... page 4
do the splits .... page 20	skip .... page 8
hop .... page 3	stand on your head ..... page 23
kick a ball .... page 6	throw a ball .... page 15
24	25

1 What page is 'kick a ball' on?   page 6

2 What is on page 3?   _____

3 What page is 'catch a ball' on?   _____

4 What page is 'do cartwheels' on?   _____

5 What is on page 15?   _____

6 What page is 'skip' on?   _____

7 What is on page 23?   _____

Remember!

We write words in an index in alphabetical order.

When the letters are the same, we look at the next letter.

shake   skip   stamp

10   Write parts of the body.

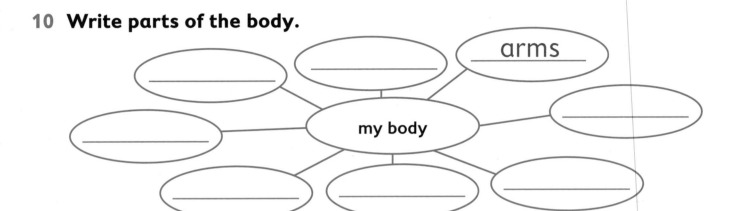

arms

my body

11   Write an index for a book about the body. Use words from Activity 5. Write the words in alphabetical order.

Index

arms _____   page 6 _____

_____   _____

_____   _____

_____   _____

_____   _____

_____   _____

_____   _____

3

My face

My face, adjectives, shapes

1 Match the two parts of the words.

1 ey ⊃ ——————— ⊂ es

2 ea ⊃   ⊂ rs

3 no ⊃   ⊂ ir

4 mou ⊃   ⊂ se

5 ha ⊃   ⊂ th

2 Complete the web. Use the words in the word box.

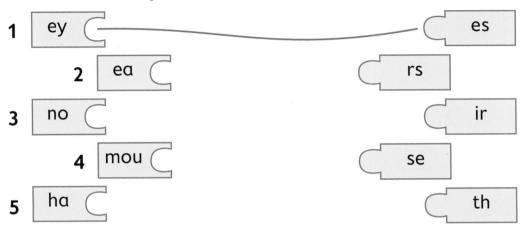

~~brown~~   ~~brown~~   blue   curly   long
straight   big   small   dark   blond

brown

hair

eyes

brown

3 Unscramble. Then match.

1 grteacnle   <u>rectangle</u>

2 tiranlge   _____

3 asuqer   _____

4 cciler   _____

a ◯

b ▢

c ▭

d △

4 Read. Then draw and colour.

1 **Me**

I've got short curly hair. It's really messy! My hair is dark. I've got big brown eyes.

2 **My friend**

My friend's got long straight hair. It's neat. My friend's hair is blond. My friend's got blue eyes.

5 Answer the questions about you.

1 Have you got long brown hair?   Yes, I have. / No, I haven't.

2 Have you got big blue eyes?   _____

3 Have you got a small nose?   _____

4 Have you got curly brown hair?   _____

6 Write new sentences.

1 Tom has got dark hair.   His hair is dark.

2 His hair is long.   He's got long hair.

3 His eyes are big.   _____

4 Lucy has got curly hair.   _____

7 **Unscramble and write. Then draw.**

| square | She's | head | a | got |

1 _____

| are | fingers | long | and | straight | Her |

2 _____

| Her | triangle | big | nose | a | is |

3 _____

8 Look. Then write sentences about the people.

Mum
Mum is on the sofa. She's got long straight hair. Her hair is neat. She's got big eyes.

Dad

My little brother

My sister

9 Read. Then circle Yes or No.

This is Anna. She's got long hair and big brown eyes.
She's got a big nose and a small mouth.

This is Ed. He's got a big nose and long hair. His hair isn't neat.
It's messy. He's got a small mouth.

This is Nick. He's got small eyes, a small nose and a small mouth.
His hair is short. His hair is dark and neat.

This is Emma. She's got short blond hair. She's got big eyes, a small
nose and a small mouth. Her ears aren't small. They're big.

1 Nick's got blond hair.	Yes / (No)	
2 Anna's nose is small.	Yes / No	
3 Emma's got big ears.	Yes / No	
4 Ed's got a big nose.	Yes / No	
5 Nick's hair is dark.	Yes / No	
6 Emma's got a big mouth.	Yes / No	

10 Read again. Then write the names.

Anna   Emma   Ed   Nick

1

2

3

4

_____   _____   _____   _____

4 Describing people

11 Write the words in the correct order.

1 brown / hair / straight

<u>straight brown hair</u>

2 eyes / blue

_____

3 hair / blond / short

_____

4 small / eyes / green

_____

12 Draw a picture or stick a photo of a face. Then circle and write.

He's/She's got _____

_____

_____

_____

_____

Animals

1 Read. Then match.

1 cow

2 goat

3 turkey

4 duck

5 hen

6 horse

a

b

c

d

e

f

2 Unscramble. Then write.

1 ksnuk

<u>s k u n k</u>

2 low

_ _ _

3 atr

_ _ _

4 bta

_ _ _

5 rlzdia

_ _ _ _ _ _

6 oxf

_ _ _

5 **What's this / that?**

3 Circle the correct words.

1 (What's)/ What are that?

2 It's / They're a turkey.

3 It's got / It's white.

4 It's got / It's feathers.

4 Look and read. Then complete.

1 <u>What's that?</u>

It's a goat.
It's big.
It's white.
It's got four legs and a tail.

2 What _____

_____
_____
_____
_____

3 _____

_____
_____
_____
_____

5 **Find and write questions and answers. Then guess the animal.**

owl ~~bat~~ hens

1 Is / big / ? / it

it / No / isn't

Is / ? / black / it

It / is / Yes

Answer

Is it big?

No, it isn't.

Is it black?

Yes, it is.

It's a bat.

2 ? / Is / big / it

it / Yes / is

big / got / Has / it / ? / eyes

it / Yes / has

Answer

_____

_____

_____

_____

_____

3 they / Are / ? / big

they / No / aren't

brown / ? / they / Are

are / Yes / they

Answer

_____

_____

_____

_____

_____

Are the ducks big?

6 Look and read. Then complete.

	duck	turkey	ostrich	cow	goat
big	✗	✔	✔	✔	✔
small	✔	✗	✗	✗	✗
brown	✗	✔	✔	✔	✗
white	✔	✗	✗	✗	✔
legs	2	2	2	4	4
wings	✔	✔	✔	✗	✗

1 The cows <u>are big and brown.</u>   <u>They've got four legs.</u>

2 The goats _____. _____

3 The turkeys _____. _____

4 The ostriches _____. _____

5 The ducks _____. _____

7 Look again. Then write and answer.

1 Q: <u>Are the ducks big?</u>   (ducks / big)

   A: <u>No, they're not. They're small.</u>

2 Q: <u>Have the turkeys got wings?</u>   (turkeys / wings)

   A: <u>Yes, they have.</u>

3 Q: _____   (ostriches / small)

   A: _____

4 Q: _____   (goats / two legs)

   A: _____

8 **What animals can you see on a farm? Think and write.**

_____

9 **What animals has Farmer Ben got on his farm? Read. Then (✔).**

Farmer Ben has got a big farm. He's got animals on his farm. Look!

What's this? It's white and it's got two black ears and four black legs. ✔

Look at that animal! It's big. It's black and white and it's got four legs and a tail.

Look at these! They're small and green. They can jump and swim. They've got thin legs and big eyes.

What's this? It's small and it's got wings and two legs. It can swim.

And look at that! It's got big wings. It can't swim. It's grey and it's got two legs. It's not a hen.

1 ✔   2 ☐   3 ☐   4 ☐

5 ☐   6 ☐   7 ☐   8 ☐

Describing animals

10 Read. Then match, colour and write.

1 This is a horse. It's big and black. It's got four legs and a long tail. It's awake in the day and asleep at night.

2 This is a _____.
It's small and brown. It's got two legs and two wings. It can't swim. It's awake in the day and asleep at night.

3 This is a _____.
It's small and grey. It's got two legs and two wings. It can fly and swim.

4 This is a _____.
It's very big and it's got big eyes. It's black and white and it's got four legs.

5 This is a _____.
It's grey. It's got four legs and a short tail. It's got big ears. It's awake in the day.

6 This is a _____.
_____
_____
_____

Food

Food

6

1 Find and circle. Then match.

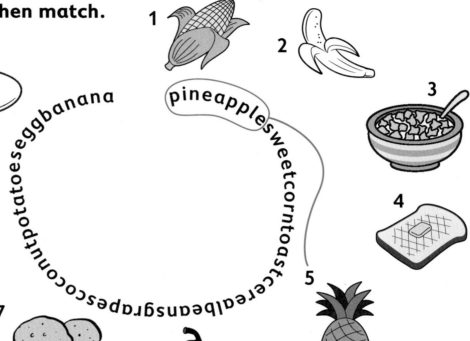

potatoeseggbanana pineapplesweetcorntoastcerealbeansgrapescoconut

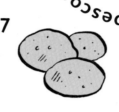

2 Unscramble. Then match.

1 ifsh   <u>f i s h</u>

2 kichcen   _ _ _ _ _ _ _

3 zipaz   _ _ _ _ _

4 dalas   _ _ _ _ _

a

b

c

d

What's your favourite food? / I like ...

3 Read. Then write the opposite.

1 I like pizza.   I don't like pizza.

2 Tom likes apples.   _____

3 Dad likes salad.   _____

4 I like chicken.   _____

4 Unscramble. Then write and answer.

1 Do / you / chicken / like / ?

   Q: Do you like chicken? _____

   A: _____

2 like / you / ? / Do / bananas

   Q: _____

   A: _____

3 mum / your / like / Does / ? / chocolate

   Q: _____

   A: _____

5 What's your favourite food? What food don't you like? Write.

_____

_____

_____

6 **Look at the food in Mum's shopping bag. Read.**
Then choose *True* (T) or *False* (F).

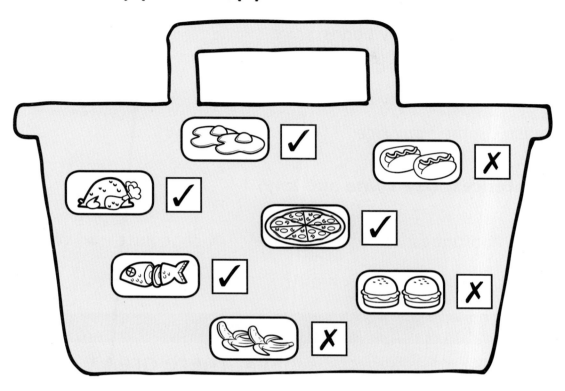

1 She likes chicken.	(T)/ F
2 She likes burgers.	T / F
3 She likes fish.	T / F
4 She doesn't like bananas.	T / F
5 She doesn't like pizza.	T / F

7 **Look again. Then write questions and answers.**

1 <u>Does Mum like bananas</u> ? <u>No</u>, <u>she doesn't</u>. (bananas)

2 _____ ? _____, _____. (hot dogs)

3 _____ ? _____, _____. (pizza)

4 _____ ? _____, _____. (eggs)

6 some / any

8 Circle *some* or *any*.

1 There's (some) / *any* milk.

2 There aren't *some* / *any* beans.

3 There are *some* / *any* pancakes.

4 There aren't *some* / *any* pineapples.

5 There isn't *some* / *any* rice.

9 Write sentences. Use *some* and *any*.

| ✔ milk   ✘ oranges   ✔ fish   ✘ honey   ✘ chocolate   ✔ vegetables |

In my kitchen ...

✔	✘
1 There's some milk _____.	2 There aren't any _____ oranges _____.
3 _____.	4 _____ _____.
5 _____.	6 _____ _____.

10 Look at the chart in Activity 9 again. Write three questions and answers.

1 Is there any honey in your kitchen?   No, there isn't.

2 _____   _____

3 _____   _____

11 What's on today's menu? Read. Then write (✔) or (✗).

Today's menu
_____

pizza
chicken
rice
fish
potatoes
bananas
pasta
pancakes

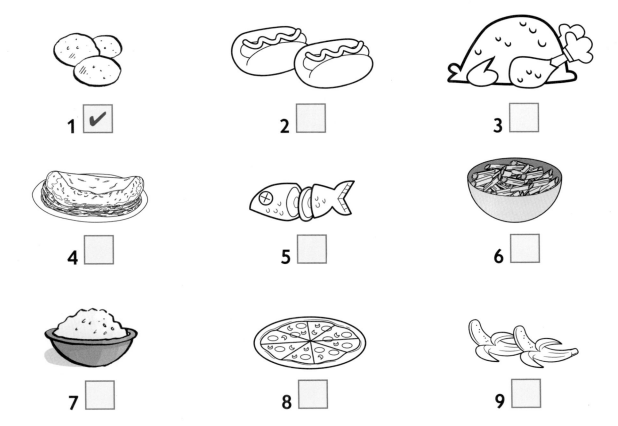

1 ✔   2 ☐   3 ☐

4 ☐   5 ☐   6 ☐

7 ☐   8 ☐   9 ☐

6 A menu

12 Write (✔) or (✗). Then correct the words which are wrong.

1 grapes   ✔   _____

2 egges   ☐   _____

3 potatos   ☐   _____

4 pineapples   ☐   _____

5 coconutes   ☐   _____

6 beans   ☐   _____

13 It's your birthday. Write a birthday menu for your friends and family.

Menu

Food	Drink

Clothes

Clothes

7

1 Match the two parts of the words.

1 sk	
2 dr	
3 sh	
4 py	
5 tr	
6 ja	

a **oes**

b **ousers**

c **ess**

d **jamas**

e **cket**

f **irt**

2 Read and write. Then match and colour.

Clothes for my holiday

1 white s <u>o c k</u> s

2 red c _ p

3 black _ oot _

4 blue je _ _ s

5 white tr _ _ n _ rs

6 grey c _ _ _ t

7 green s _ i _ t

8 yellow j _ _ _ p _ r

a

b

c

d

e

f **1**

g

h

3 Look and write.

1   2   3   4

1   I'm a firefighter. I'm ___wearing___ a helmet. I'm ___not wearing___ a cap.

2   I'm a police officer. I'm _____ a shirt.
I'm _____ a jacket.

3   I'm a chef. I'm _____ a skirt. I'm _____ trousers.

4   I'm a nurse. I'm _____ shoes. I'm _____ trainers.

4 You are at school. What are you wearing? Draw. Then write.

I'm wearing _____
_____
_____
_____
_____

5 You are on holiday. What are you wearing? Draw. Then write.

_____
_____
_____
_____
_____

6 Unscramble. Then answer about you.

1 you / ? / Are / wearing / skirt / today / a

Q: <u>Are you wearing a skirt today?</u>

A: _____

2 black / wearing / ? / Are / shoes / you

Q: _____

A: _____

3 jumper / green / ? / wearing / you / Are / a

Q: _____

A: _____

7 What are you wearing? Write (✔) or (✗). Then write sentences.

T-shirt	☐	shoes	☐	jeans	☐
coat	☐	jumper	☐	dress	☐
trainers	☐	skirt	☐	cap	☐
trousers	☐	socks	☐	pyjamas	☐

1 ✔ <u>I'm wearing a dress.</u>

2 ✗ <u>I'm not wearing</u> _____

3 ✔ _____

4 ✗ _____

5 ✔ _____

7 What would you like?

8 Unscramble and write. Then answer about you.

| blue | Would | like | coat | a | ? | you |

1 Q: Would you like a blue coat?

A: _____

| shoes | like | Would | ? | you | black |

2 Q: _____

A: _____

9 Read the list. Then complete the conversation.

grey skirt   like   wouldn't   thank you   ~~would~~   white socks

1 What **would** you like?

2 I'd _____ a shirt, please.

3 Would you like some _____?

4 No, I _____ thank you.

5 Would you like a _____?

6 Yes, I would, _____.

10 Read. Then number and colour.

1

Hi, I'm Amy. I'm wearing a long red dress and black shoes. I'm not wearing socks.

2

I'm Tom. I'm wearing a purple jumper and blue jeans. I'm not wearing shoes but I'm wearing green socks.

3

I'm Kelly. I'm wearing a green skirt, an orange T-shirt and brown boots. I'm wearing glasses.

4

And that's Bob. He's wearing yellow pyjamas and yellow socks. He isn't wearing any shoes.

a

Bob

b

Kelly

1

c

Amy

d

Tom

7 Describing clothes

11 Read. Then correct.

1 Where are my pyjama?

Where are my pyjamas?

2 Your jean are on the bed.

_____

3 Your trainer are here.

_____

4 My glasses is in my bag.

_____

12 What clothes would you like? Think and write.

- Do you like your friend's clothes?
- Would you like Charlie's and Rose's clothes?
- Would you like a famous person's clothes?

I'd like _____

_____

_____

_____

Weather

Weather, activities

1 **Look at the weather symbols. Then write.**

1  It's __snowy__.

2 It's _____.

3 It's _____.

4 It's _____.

5 It's _____.

6 It's _____.

2 **Look and match.**

1 take a photo

2 read a book

3 make a snowman

4 go for a walk

5 ride a bike

6 fly a kite

a

b

c

d

e

f

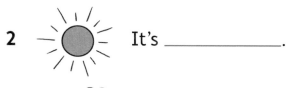

What's the weather like?

3 Look at the pictures. Then complete the conversations.

1

What's the weather like?

It's windy.

2

What's the weather like?

_____

3

What's the weather like?

_____

4

_____ the weather _____?

_____

5

_____

_____

4 Unscramble. Then write.

1 weather / What's / like / the / December / ? / in

<u>What's the weather like in December?</u>

2 cold / is / It / wet / and

_____

3 your / ? / weather / What's / favourite

_____

4 favourite / month / is / ? / Which / your

_____

5 Read and answer for you. Then draw.

1 Do you like windy days?

<u>Yes, I do. I like windy days.</u>

2 Do you like rainy days?

_____

3 Do you like sunny days?

_____

4 Do you like snowy days?

_____

8   This kite is mine

6   Read, think and complete. Use words from the word box.

> hers   ~~mine~~   yours   mine   yours

It's windy today. I can fly my kite.
Look – this kite is <u>mine</u>.
It's red and yellow. Hey, Tom!
That's Sue's kite. It's blue and white. It isn't _____.
It's _____! _____ is red and orange.
I think _____ is the most beautiful!

7   Unscramble and write.

1   kite / mine / This / is
   <u>This kite is mine.</u>

2   is / snowman / That / yours
   _____

3   These / keys / are / hers
   _____

4   is / This / pencil case / hers
   _____

5   mine / These / hot dogs / are
   _____

8   Write questions and answers. Use the prompts.

1   <u>Do you like cloudy days?</u> (cloudy days)   <u>No, I don't.</u> (✗)

2   _____ (hot days)   _____ (✔)

3   _____ (windy days)   _____ (✗)

9 Read. Who likes cold days?

Wednesday 4th December

It's cold and snowy today. I like snowy days! I can make a snowman and take photos with my camera. I can wear my blue coat. I can read my book and watch TV. December is my favourite month. It's cold. I love cold days!

Emily

Wednesday 4th December

Today it's freezing! I don't like cold days! I don't like December. I don't want to make a snowman. I like warm and sunny days. I want to go for a walk, ride my bike and fly a kite. August is my favourite month. August is hot!

Kevin

10 Read again. Then write *E* = Emily or *K* = Kevin.

1 I want to make a snowman.   E

2 I like snowy days.   ☐

3 I want to fly a kite.   ☐

4 My favourite month is December.   ☐

5 I want to go for a walk.   ☐

6 I've got a camera.   ☐

8 A diary

Remember!

In diaries, we usually write the date at the top.

Monday 6th July

11 Write a diary entry for January. Then write a diary entry for July.

- What's the weather like today?
- Do you like cold / rainy / sunny / warm days?
- What can you do today?
- What can't you do today?
- What's your favourite weather?

Tuesday 21st January

Today it's _____

_____

_____

_____

_____

_____

_____

_____

Friday 17th July

Today it's _____

_____

_____

_____

_____

_____

_____

_____